Retriever Labrador:

Retriever Labrador are large dogs, with a height of up to 60 centimeters. They are larger than most dogs, but they are not as large as dogs of giant races, such as St. Bernard.

Retriever Labrador:

Retriever Labrador have short and dense. The hair can be black, yellow or chocolate. Retriever Labrador have an inner layer of hair that helps them stay warm in winter and an outer layer of hair protects them from rain and sun.

Retriever Labrador:

Personality The Labrador Retiever are very affectionate dogs and love to play. They are great companions for children and other people. Retriever Labrador are also very intelligent and easy to train. They can learn to make a lot of tricks, such as sitting, bedtime and giving the paw.

Retriever Labrador:

Uses Retriever Labrador are very versatile dogs. They are used as company dogs, therapy dogs, assistance dogs and work dogs. Retriever Labrador are very good swimmers and are often used as water rescue dogs.

German shepherd:

Do you want a protective, obedient and always alert dog? German pastors are known for their intelligence, loyalty and protective nature. They are excellent guard and service dogs.

German shepherd:

German shepherds have long and dense hair. The hair can be black, brown or yellow. German shepherds have a sub-service that helps keep them warm in winter and an outer layer of hair that protects them from rain and sun.

German shepherd:

Personality German shepherds are very intelligent and affectionate dogs. They are very loyal to their owners and love to protect them. German pastors are also very active and need a lot of exercise.

German shepherd:

Uses German shepherds are very versatile dogs. They are used as company dogs, police dogs, service dogs, agility dogs and obedience dogs. German shepherds are also great swimmers and are often used as water rescue dogs.

Poodle:

Do you want a smart and playful dog, perfect for exposure or work?Poodles are known for their intelligence and playful nature. Th are excellent exposure and work dogs.

Poodle:

Size Poodles come in four sizes standard, medium, dwarf and toy. The standard poodles are the largest, measuring up to 60 centimeters high. Middle poodles measure between 35 and 45 centimeters. The miniature poodles measure between 28 and 35 centimeters. Toy Poodles measure less than 28 centimeters.

Poodle:

Coat Poodles have a curly coat that can be of any color, including black, brown, white, cream or red. Poodles's hair does not fall as much as that of other dog breeds, which makes them a good choice for people with allergies.

Poodle:

Poodles are very intelligent and easy to train dogs. They are very affectionate and love to play. Poodles are also very active and need a lot of exercise.

Poodle:

Uses Poodles are used as company dogs, therapy dogs, assistance dogs and work dogs. Poodles are also great swimmers and are usually used as water rescue dogs.

French bulldog

They are very affectionate and love to be with people. French bulldogs are very sociable dogs and love to be close to their owners. They love to play, hug and receive affection.

French bulldog

They are very intelligent and easy to train. French bulldogs are very intelligent dogs and learn tricks and commands quickly. They are a good option for families with children, as they can learn to sit, giving pads and more.

French bulldog

They are small, which makes them ideal for living in apartments. French bulldogs are small dogs, so they don't need much room to live. They are a good option for families who live in apartments or small houses.

French bulldog

They don't need much exercise. French bulldogs are calm dogs and don't need much exercise. A daily walk or a joke in the park is enough to keep them happy and healthy.

Beagle

Detective nose! Beagles have a superpowered nose that allows them to smell things you can't even imagine. They are like muzzle detectives, they can follow a trail of smells for kilometers!

Beagle

Infinite energy. These puppies are like living ping pong balls! They love running, playing and jumping all day. They are always ready for an adventure and will keep it active.

Beagle

Musical howl. They don't bark like the other dogs, the beagles howled! Your howl is like a beautiful and sad song at the same time. Some love it, others find it funny!

Beagle

Friends of all. Beagles are very sociable and friendly. They love to play with other dogs, children and even the hairy cats. They are always looking for new friends to have fun!

Boxer

Champion energy! Boxers are like small athletes, always full of energy and ready to play. They love running, jumping and kissing you with all enthusiasm. Get ready for an adventure companion!

Boxer

Giant stuffed heart. Behind their strong appearance, the boxers have a huge heart. They are very loving and protectors with their families, especially with children. They love to snuggle to watch a movie or hug you after a long day.

Boxer

Famous players. There is nothing that boxers love more than playing. They love balls, cable games and anything that keeps them active. They are amazing companions for outdoor fun.

Boxer

Always smiling. Look at the face of a boxer, he always seems to be smiling! His cheerful and playful expression will make him happy in a moment.

English bulldog

They are very affectionate! English Bulldogs are very sociable dogs and love to be close to their owners. They love to play, hug and receive affection.

English bulldog

They are very loyal! English bulldogs are very protective dogs of their families and are always available to take care of them. They are amazing companions for children and adults.

English bulldog

They are very funny! English Bulldogs have a very peculiar facial expression that always makes us smile. Also, they love to do mischief and play.

English bulldog

They don't need much exercise! English bulldogs are calm dogs and don't need much exercise. A daily walk or a joke in the park is enough to keep them happy and healthy.

Pug

Wrinkled and happy face Look what a face full of wrinkles! Pugs have a unique expression that always looks happy, even when they are sleeping. They are like plush bears with mustaches.

Pug

Callous hugs Pugs love to snuggle and kiss. They are perfect companions for movie nights or to read a book on the couch. They are always ready for a warm hug!

Pug

Champion snoring Pugs are known for their lovely snoring. They sound like small engines and sometimes even seem to hum a song. Don't worry, it's just their way to say they are comfortable and happy!

Pug

Playful friends Pugs love to play, especially with balls and other toys. They are very active and curious, always in search of the next adventure. They will keep you entertained with your mischief!

Chihuahua

Little Giants! Chihuahuas are the smallest dogs in the world, but have a huge personality. They are brave, bold and always ready to defend their family!

Chihuahua

Voice singing! Do not trust your size. The chihuahuas have a tall and high bark that can surprise you. They are like small trumpets with legs!

Chihuahua

Pocket hug! Despite their brave attitude, the chihuahuas love hugs and caresses. They are like stuffed balls that fit perfectly in their arms. Get ready for many hugs!

Chihuahua

Adventure without stopping! The chihuahuas are curious and full of energy. They love to explore, play and walk. They are always ready for a new adventure, whether in the park or at home!

Shih Tzu

Silk coat Shih tzus has long, beautiful silk coats. It's like a waterfall of hair running down your body. They come in many different colors, such as white, black, brown and gold!

Shih Tzu

Plush smiles Shih tzus love to play and have fun. They always have a smile on their face, even when they are sleeping. Your happy expression is contagious and will make you smile too!

Shih Tzu

Love Friends Shih Tzus are very sociable and love to be close to people. They are amazing companions for children and love affection and hugs. They are always there to give you a lick in the face and make you feel loved!

Shih Tzu

Easy to train Shih tzus are smart dogs and love learning tricks. They are relatively easy to train, which makes them a good choice for families with children. You can teach your Shih Tzu to swing the paw, sit or even wave with your head!

Pomerania

They are very small! Pomeranians are the smallest dogs in the family of Spitz dogs. Adults weigh between 1.4 and 3.2 kg.

Pomerania

They have a great personality! Pomeranians are very playful, outgoing, intelligent, sociable and friendly. They love children and are always ready to play.

Pomerania

They have for the beautiful! Pomeranians have a soft, soft coat that can be of various colors, including white, black, blue, red, brown, gray and cream.

Pomerania

They are easy to take care of! Pomeranians require regular brushing to keep the coat clean and healthy. They also need daily walks and games to stay active.

Yorkshire Terrier

They are very small! Yorkshire Terriers are the smallest dogs of the Terrier family. Adults weigh between 2.5 and 3.2 kg.

Yorkshire Terrier

They have a great personality! Yorkshire Terriers are very intelligent, active, loyal and protectors. They love to be with their owners and are always ready to play.

Yorkshire Terrier

They have for the beautiful! Yorkshire terriers have long, silky hair that can be blue or gold.

Yorkshire Terrier

They are easy to take care of! Yorkshire Terriers require regular brushing to keep the coat clean and healthy. They also need daily walks and games to stay active.

Dachshund

They are very long! Dachshunds have a long, short -legged body. They are like sausages with legs!

Dachshund

They have a great personality! Dachshunds are very intelligent, active, curious and loyal. They love to be with their owners and are always ready to explore.

Dachshund

They are loving! Dachshunds love hugs and hugs. They love to be close to their owners and are always present to kiss or a hug.

Dachshund

They are easy to take care of! Dachshunds require regular brushing to keep the coat clean and healthy. They also need daily walks and games to stay active.

Italian greyhound

They are very fast! The Italian Galcos are hunting dogs and are known for their speed. They can run at speeds of up to 60 km/h.

Italian greyhound

They are very affectionate! The Italian Galcos are very affectionate dogs and love to be with their owners. They are very

Italian greyhound

They are easy to take care of! Italian Galcos do not require much maintenance. They only need regular brushing and daily walks.

Italian greyhound

They are very adaptable! Italian gamns can live in apartments or houses. They are very adaptable to different environments.

English setter

They are very affectionate! English setters love to be with their owners and love hugs and affection.

English setter

They are very intelligent! English Setters are easy to train and can learn a lot of tricks.

English setter

They are very active! English setters need a lot of exercise, so they need daily walks and outdoor games.

English setter

They are very good with children! English setters are patient and affectionate to children and love to play.

ROTTWEILER

They are very intelligent! Rottweilers are very intelligent and easy to train dogs. They can learn tricks and obey orders.

ROTTWEILER

They are very protective! Rottweilers are very protective dogs of their owners and their families. They are very good at protecting yours.

ROTTWEILER

They are very affectionate! Rottweilers are very affectionate dogs and love to be with their owners. They are very good neck dogs.

ROTTWEILER

They are very easy to take care! Rottweilers do not require much maintenance. They only need regular brushing and daily walks.

Siberian Husky

They are very active! Siberian Huskies need a lot of exercise, so they need daily walks and outdoor games.

Siberian Husky

They are very intelligent! Siberian Huskies are easy to train and can learn many tricks.

Siberian Husky

They are very affectionate! Siberian Huskies are very affectionate dogs and love to be with their owners.

Siberian Husky

They are so beautiful! Siberian huskies have thick and cute hair that comes in a variety of colors including black, white, brown and red.